ANNIS WOULD

AND WE KNOW

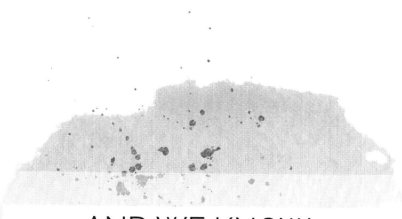

AND WE KNOW

ANNIS WOULD

ANNIS WOULD

DEDICATION

My life has been formed by Jesus and a deep love of story.
I credit my Aunt Althea for my deep roots in both.

Tee Tee, this one is for you.

I love you.

CONTENTS

INTRODUCTION

HOW DO YOU KNOW?

"But HOW do you KNOW?" Rose's face was bright red and wet with tears.

For the record, Rose was a respectful girl who was usually very levelheaded. Wise for her age, she often used words like "facetious" appropriately. She was also currently ruffling her hands through her hair as if ready to pull it out in tufts.

Rose did not believe that the number 110 existed. Having attended kindergarten for a week, she was confident that she understood numbers better than I could.

The whole ordeal began with her homework.

Water was boiling on the stove. Groceries sat waiting for me to put them away. So when Rose excitedly asked me to listen to her count by 10s, I had distractedly agreed. As I decided whether to freeze the chicken or put it in the refrigerator, I listened to her little voice authoritatively rattle off "70, 80, 90, 100, 120..."

I almost didn't notice what was missing.

"Hey, Rose," I called from the kitchen as I began cutting some carrots. "Can you count that again?"

Eagerly, she listed off the numbers. "90, 100, 120..."

In her eagerness, she made it to 150 before I put down my knife and called over my shoulder again, "But Rose, what about 110?"

"Annis, there is no 110."

My brow furrowed. I walked into the dining room, "Why do you say that?" I asked. She looked at me as if she was about to explain something quite simple to a child.

"That's how numbers work, Annis. We learned to count by ones first. Numbers go '1, 2, 3, 4, 5, 6, 7, 8, 9,' and then it starts over. You don't have two "10s" in a row." She laid her palms out face up, as if her evidence resolved the matter.

She had me stumped for a moment. I could understand her logic—why, when one is counting by tens would there be two tens right in a row? It was silly.

I briefly imagined the rest of her life from this moment. Years of taxes, purchases and deposits all made without the number 110. I supposed it was a life that was possible. I began to wonder how many times I encountered 110 in my daily life.

Yup. I'll admit it. I almost justified not having the argument based on the fact that the child would 'get by okay' without us talking about it.

I internally sighed. I was a nanny. I knew this was my job. I gave myself a pep talk—I could do this. I could explain it to her.

But five minutes later I stood, arms crossed, in front of an indignant kindergartner who had asked a very valid question.

How do you know?

I huffed. I couldn't think of how to explain how I knew there was 110. I was 19, which put me too close to childhood to bring myself to say, "Because I said so." She was right—I should know how I knew.

I distinctly remember pinching my nose. It seemed like the moment in a conversation when an adult would pinch their nose.

I continued, "I have been in kindergarten. I have graduated elementary school. I have gone to middle school and high school, and I am currently in college. Unless numbers have drastically changed since last semester, I can assure you: there is an 110."

Translation: I'm smarter than you and more experienced than you, and that automatically makes me right.

In hindsight, it is no surprise that we lasted maybe another five minutes before we both went to our separate corners. We agreed we would talk with Mom about it when she got home.

One of the benefits of Rose being five is her emotional rebound rate was rather high. Five minutes later, she and her younger sister were re-enacting Cinderella over broccoli and chicken fingers.

As they played together, their mother returned home. I caught her up on the day as she unloaded her briefcase onto the kitchen island.

More than once we had shared shaken heads and a quiet, "These kids, am I right?" I think I was expecting the same exchange to repeat in this instance. Instead, she gave me a slightly amused smile as she heard me explain the confusion over 110.

She threw a glance in her daughter's direction as she chuckled. She flipped through a file, saying, "It's funny, isn't it? How much we take for granted knowing what we know?"

It is funny. What happened next is kind of funny, too.

I hopped into my car and drove home, thinking about the battle that lay ahead for Rose's parents.

But I didn't leave them to a fight. There were no tears or pulled out hair. Instead, they had a simple, one-minute conversation with their daughter.

They used Rose's piggy bank.

Rose was an avid reader. She would save the money she received from each birthday card, the tooth fairy and various chores in her piggy bank until the next trip to the bookstore. She understood that ten dimes were the same allowance as four quarters or one dollar.

Rose's parents had her take out two one-dollar bills from her piggy bank. When her father tried to trade nineteen dimes for her two dollars, Rose very quickly became convinced that 110 did, in fact, exist.

Rose's parents knew their daughter well. They knew what Rose knew and what she did not. They compassionately remembered not knowing.

I am no longer 19. I left "teendom" many years ago. I no longer nanny Rose and her sister. But this experience has tarred and feathered me. It is a situation that quickly comes to mind when I am asked about other things that matter, other areas in which I will be seen as an authority whether I am prepared or not.

Often, this area is faith. Many times I avoid certain serious conversations for the same reason I almost avoided the topic of 110 with Rose. "They'll get by," I think.

I'll avoid dialogue because it will be challenging, or I'll jump into a debate—prepared to defend my opinion rather than to share my knowledge.

It is so important to equip ourselves to be ready for these dialogues, particularly in the arena of faith. When we are asserting the reason for our life and existence, we have to understand what it is. We sell ourselves short if we don't. It is the foundation our faith builds on, and the starting point of how our faith shapes our lives.

Many Bible verses underline God's desire to be known by us. In Matthew 16, Jesus asks His disciples who the people say that He is. They answer with an assortment of titles, such as "teacher" or "prophet."

He then presses in further, with possibly one of the most challenging questions posed to the disciples. "Who do you say that I am?"

Peter responds with vigor, saying, "You are the Messiah, the Son of the living God."

Jesus responds with a blessing; He tells Peter that He will build His Church upon Peter's understanding, that all the powers of hell will not conquer it.

So, it seems this understanding is more than a little bit important. It's vital.

However, so often we copy-and-paste our answers from sermons and devotionals and verses. Don't get me wrong, that information is a fantastic reference for our faith. However, it is not the answer for our faith.

We're going to spend the rest of our time together talking about what is.

HOW *DO* I KNOW?

Now, you're probably asking me the same question that Rose wailed to me, "How do you know?"

It is as fair of a question as it is old. We ask this question in different ways throughout our days, weeks, years and lives. As we are always seeking truth and trying to relate to facts, this issue is a fundamental building block to our learning.

When someone asks 'how' and we have forgotten the not-knowing, we are being invited to remember how we learned.

As with lawyers and professors, it is never enough for a witness or student to rattle off opinions. We have to be able to explain how we know and prove where we learned it.

However, there is a fine line to tread here. We can't copy down source material verbatim. That's cheating; that's plagiarism!

To copy and paste someone else's words weakens the integrity of our argument because it doesn't prove that we understand or believe what we are claiming. We show our "knowing" by stating what we have learned in terms, phrases and experiences that are our own.

When we copy and paste our answers to questions regarding faith from sermons, books and apologetics courses but do not interact with the truth of it, we are plagiarizing faith. We cheapen eternity. If we begin to make claims about knowledge but do not engage with the truth of them, it becomes much easier to speak out of turn.

It is a big and important idea, as is often the case with things that matter. I have found that the easiest way to teach big ideas is often to simplify.

To begin with our simplification, I'm going to start with a big, impressive word. Of course.

The word is 'epistemology'. Isn't it delightful? I feel smarter just saying it, and it's a solid 19 points in Scrabble.

According to Merriam-Webster:

EPISTEMOLOGY *NOUN*

epis·te·mol·o·gy \i-ˌpis-tə-ˈmä-lə-jē\

The study or a theory of the nature and grounds of knowledge especially concerning its limits and validity

The textbook definition would elaborate, saying that epistemology is an investigation into what separates justified belief from opinion. To shorten, it is the study of how we know what we know, and what separates our knowledge from what we think. To simplify even further, epistemology is the study of what makes something verifiably true.

By definition, information without accountability isn't knowledge. The root of the word knowledge is 'know' (or gno). Another word with the same root is ignore, which communicates the real meaning of 'gno': an intentional consideration rather than a regurgitation of information.

By this root definition, knowing is to have believed and confirmed. It is similar to the experience detailed in early Genesis when Adam and Eve's eyes are open for knowledge beyond the mere sight they had before. Prior to eating from the tree, they saw; after eating from the tree they began to comprehend. What about us? We have seen, but do we *know*?

CAN I GET A WITNESS?

I promised to make things simple, and here is where we hit it. Rudimentary journalism and the courtroom share many commonalities, both being areas where investigators examine pieces of evidence in the pursuit of truth.

Using the investigative vocabulary common in writing classes and an attorney's defense, we are going to dig in and study our knowledge. It will then equip us to be aware of our understanding and then prioritize what information to share when we're asked, "How do you know?"

Remember Rose? She didn't want my educational pedigree or my current resume. She only wanted the facts.

Lucky for us, this investigative vernacular features the same basic information-gathering questions we learned from infancy. These are among the first phrases taught in a foreign language class and the bullet points of police investigations. I'm talking about the 5 W's.

WHO, WHAT, WHEN, WHERE AND WHY.

Think about it. These words cover the basics in obtaining necessary information. They help us understand any situation and its context. Understanding that, we won't go too deeply into the given circumstances. This book isn't a study to know what you don't; it's a study of how to know what you know.

I hope this book is different than others you read. I have no interest in telling you what to think; I want to make sure you are equipped to know what you know and think for yourself. It is my hope these foundations will help you go deeper into your faith so you may feel confident and secure.

While I'll give you examples and evidence in the typical courtroom format, I'm going to take a page from my favorite theologian. Like Jesus, I'm going to tell you stories.

With our scene set, let the story begin.

WHO

CHRISTMAS, 1997

It began in October. I remember it clearly. At the age of eight, as soon as I had decided what my Halloween costume was going to be, I was ready for Christmas.

Especially this year. I was certain I would soon have my own Nintendo 64. I had spent the past year badgering my cousins to let me play a couple of rounds (or fifteen) of Mario Kart every time we visited their house. I watched with envy as they made progress through Zelda; I wasn't allowed to make the commitment of starting a game I wouldn't have the opportunity to finish.

I spent the autumn months hinting with as much subtlety as a jackhammer. Ten days after Halloween, my dad asked me for my Christmas list. "Finally," I thought. I remember tearing off the perforated edges from my ripped notebook page. I pulled out a teal gel pen, and not wanting to appear desperate, listed a Nintendo 64 as item number three.

"And a purple controller...if you don't mind," I scrawled in the margins.

Of course, being eight years old, I continued my heavy-handed hints. I began to wax poetic about the odd jobs I would do around the house to finance my soon-to-be gaming habit. This practice went on for about two weeks. We were driving to church, and I was offering to paint the kitchen cabinets when my dad sighed. The sigh was a bit excessive for my tastes.

"Oh no," I thought. My dad sighing was never a good sign. It signaled the quickly approaching death of a dream he had deemed impractical.

"Well, Annis," he said, sighing again for good measure. "I want to prepare you. You're getting older. I want to invest in your future. So your presents this year..." He paused as he took a left-hand turn into the parking lot, "They might be more educational."

He put the car in park. "Now, Squirrel," he continued, using his favorite nickname for me, "I know you love to learn!" He ruffled my hair. "I just want you to meet your full potential."

Yes, I did love to learn. I was the runner-up in the spelling bee, after all! But I was eight years old. The last thing I wanted to hear from my dad was my Christmas gifts were going to be educational; he might as well have told me he had cancelled Christmas entirely.

My dad's car door slammed, and I jumped in surprise, having been lost in my thoughts. I quickly unbuckled my seatbelt and jumped out of the car. Doubt began sneaking its way into my mind.

For the first time in my life, I began to loosen my grip on hope. Instead, I started preparing myself for disappointment.

Christmas morning came. Despite myself, I woke with high anticipation before the sun rose. I excitedly ran downstairs to unload my stocking. Then came the traditional sitting on my hands until the clock rolled to 6:30 am.

Then I could wake up my father. Then I would finally know what was hiding inside the carefully wrapped packages under the tree.

I examined the tree, skimming over every gift underneath its branches. My eyes landed on one box, strategically placed toward the back of the tree. "Just the right size," I thought, beginning to feel a small measure of anticipation. Maybe? Could it be?

The first cracks of sunlight came peeking through the trees in our front yard. The moment the clock read 6:30 I tiptoed up the stairs, curled my fingers around the doorframe and leaned eagerly into my Dad's room, whispering as I did every Christmas morning.

"Daddy. It's Christmas!"

All I could see was his hair sticking out from under his comforter. At my whisper, I saw him begin to shuffle awake. I excitedly turned to pad back down the stairs with eager feet. I wondered, briefly, if I should have made him coffee. It was the first time the thought had occurred to me, but I realized that it would have been a kind thing to do. I was quickly distracted by the excitement beginning to shake through my body.

He softly meandered down the stairs, purposefully slow, holding me in anticipation as I waited to open my gifts. He trudged over to the video camera so he could film the occasion. We began our gift unwrapping process, first me, then him, back and forth, trading presents like the rhythm of a rocking chair, back and forth, back and forth.

Then, only one gift remained for me. I had saved it for last; of *course,* I saved it for last.

I looked at my father with expectation, sliding one finger under the wrapping paper with uncharacteristic care. I painstaking undid the tape, my breath catching as the paper slid away to reveal...a rock tumbler.

What? Everything went silent as I stared at the gift. A plastic "toy" designed to take dirty, rough stones and polish them into bright, shiny gems. In other words, not an N64. I was barely aware of my dad saying something, talking about how I had pointed one out to him when we had walked through a toy store a few months ago.

It was a toy store, I thought. **Everything** *looks cool in a toy store.*

Dad went into the kitchen to freshen up his coffee. As I have watched many times, the home video of this moment shows me sitting in a nest of blankets, staring at my gift in a stupor. I began reading the sides of the box, hoping I could talk myself into feeling the same enthusiasm I had for the hoped-for Nintendo 64. As I skimmed the text, I saw the small script on the side of the box that read, "Polishes your finds into gems in as little as a month!"

My dad came back into the living room, stirring his coffee and looking at the tree.

"Hey, Annis."

I grunted, continuing to process. *"...in as little as a month."* Did that mean it could take more than a month?

"Annis, come here. Did the cat knock down an ornament?"

I shook myself slightly from my daze. I didn't even consider my dad could pluck a fallen ornament from the tree himself.

I trudged over, annoyance souring my mood.

"Where, Dad?" I peered into the tree. *Can't you tell I'm trying to be happy with what you gave me?*

"Look here!" He pointed again, right where I was looking. I also pointed, even though I saw nothing.

"Lower!" He began to get oddly excited. I knelt down, reaching into the tree. My hand connected with something solid, but it wasn't an ornament; the shape was wrong. What I held felt like a thin, small box. My brow furrowed as I pulled it out.

The box was gift-wrapped, but it was exactly the right size.

I looked up at him, shocked. "Um...is this...?" I muttered, confused.

Dad tried to keep a straight face, but his eyes had lit up like the Fourth of July. He smiled over his coffee. "Open it."

Now is probably an appropriate time to tell you that my entire family loves Christmas. We have all considered that we might be descended from elves. As such, I've grown up on many Christmas specials, including the popular one where a main character desperately wants a BB gun for Christmas. It is one of my father's favorites, and apparently, he had long dreamed of recreating the climactic scene. In the film, the hero's father hid the desperately desired gift just out of view, surprising his child at the last moment.

I'm no authority on these matters, but I would say that he pulled it off.

I ripped away the wrapping paper to reveal one corner of MarioKart 64. Shock flooded my body. My gaze snapped up to meet his. "Is it downstairs?" I asked incredulously.

He sipped his coffee again. "Only one way for you to find out," he winked, grinning at the funny look on my face.

I flew down the stairs, rounding the corner to see an entire N64 system already set up, complete with two controllers (one gray and one *purple)* and three more games.

I promptly did what any child would do in that situation. *I lost my mind.*

I'm confident that people heard my screams of joy in the next time zone. It took me at least two minutes of jumping around for joy like a crazy person before I called up the stairs, "Well, are we gonna play or what?!"

We were three races into the Flower Cup before I remembered the promise he had made weeks prior. "I thought I was only getting educational toys this year," I curiously questioned my dad.

He shrugged, laughter filling his voice as he said, "Video games build hand-eye coordination."

Then he launched a green turtle shell at my character as I crossed the finish line, and I crowed with glee.

In this story, I didn't know my father's character very well. Therefore, my expectations of Christmas morning did not match the reality of who he was.

Now, to be fair, I was eight years old. Further, I was a fairly literal eight-year-old. I took pretty much everything at face value. Now as a (hopefully) more mature adult, I look back at my assumption I wouldn't enjoy or appreciate what my father had determined would be good for me. I created those expectations without considering my dad's character or what I knew about him.

With this frame of reference, let's fast forward a bit.

FIFTEEN YEARS LATER

One night during late summer, my dad and I were up late talking. We took turns updating each other about our lives. Reruns of one of my favorite shows played in the background.

Then he asked me a question.

"If someone asked you about me, what would you say?"

Caught off guard, I stopped to think. My dad doesn't usually ask for affirmation. The funny thing is, I'm usually pretty eager to talk about how awesome my dad is.

For example, shortly after this conversation, the lead costume coordinator for my high school theater department, Christine, sent my dad a message on Facebook. She typed, "I just need to send you a quick note to say your daughter truly loves you. She talks about you all the time. Our conversations always seem to come back to how much she appreciates being yours."

It's true. My father's praises are frequently on my lips. I just don't usually actually tell him those things.

Isn't that how it goes?

Now I had to figure out how to answer my dad's question. I considered the right words for a moment, choosing which phrases would best communicate what felt impossible to express adequately.

"Well, first I would ask if they have a spare hour," I started, smiling. "But I would, and have, told others about how you love me. How you gave up or lost pretty much everything for me: your marriage, your dream home, your reputation, our dog and so much money." Tears pricked the corners of my eyes as I looked at him. "You have always been in my corner, putting me before yourself and never once counting the cost."

Memories began to flood my mind. I continued, "I'd tell them about how you wouldn't talk when I was upset. You'd just put a record on the turntable and let me dance on top of the coffee table."

I smiled, remembering the scratching sound of the needle hitting vinyl and the gentle static before U2 filled the room. We danced until the record played out, panting from the effort. "There is nothing," my dad proclaimed, "that prayer and a dance party can't fix."

My mouth continued to move, but I was losing myself in the memories I was sharing. The family vacations that consisted of hopping on the next flight out, renting a car and then driving until we found a hotel that looked promising. So many adventures.

"I would tell them about your unique method of training me in being honest," I laughed out loud. My dad smirked. His approach to teaching honesty is what I like to call the 'noose' method. He would start with a vague confrontation, usually asking me about an expectation we had previously agreed on.

"Annis," he would say, "you remember you are grounded from TV, right?" The words would hit my ears like thick rope landing on my shoulders. Then I would give him a vague, non-committal answer, hoping the conversation would go elsewhere. He would relentlessly continue questioning me.

Lovingly, he gave me opportunity after opportunity to confess until I finally had told him enough half-truths to fess up. His method shaped me and also influenced how I confronted others. It directly informed my nannying style to boot.

"I would say how you have always been honest about your struggles and failures," I continued. "I can count the number of times you made a show of authority on one hand." In reality, I could count them on three fingers, and his restraint taught me more than any show of force would have. "The lessons that stuck with me the most were single sentences that started with you telling me, 'I am your father, but I'm also a man.'"

It's true. And I meant it. "I am your father, but I am also a man. I want someone to love you for what is beneath your face, not what is on it." My dad's words still ring through my mind whenever I get ready for a night out. "I am your father, but I'm also a man. I want you to be loved for who you are, not for how you make a guy feel." These words kept me out of many immature situations and experiences. They were reminders not to allow myself to be defined by desire; men could—and *should*—hold me in esteem.

As I remembered all of this, I began to get flustered. I couldn't express everything I wanted to say. How loving my father is. How kind and faithful he has been. There simply weren't enough words in my vocabulary. I tried to continue, words falling over each other as I told my father, "The best of me comes from you." Not because he's an extraordinary man, but because he has always taken exceptional care to point me to Christ.

After at least 20 minutes, I finally paused to take a breath. Dad took the pause to interject, saying unexpectedly, "Well, you have more than proven my point."

That's when I remembered: Right. Dad had asked a weird question. It's basically "Dad code" to ask an odd question that leads to a teaching moment.

He continued, "When describing me, what did you lead with? Did you start with, 'Oh, he didn't let me get my license until I was 18,' or 'He would punish me by grounding me from my books...?'"

"No! I talked about your love, Dad! You loved me by training me." I assure you, as the only child of a single father, I got away with nothing.

He nodded. "You did. You led with my love."

Then, he paused. Which, in Dad language, is usually code for, "Buckle up, Squirrel, there's more!"

"Maybe we have done God a disservice by leading with the rules," Dad said next. "Yes, there are rules, but the rules are not the most important—what is most important is there is a Father Who greatly loves all of us."

A MATTER OF CONTEXT

I wish I could accurately communicate the full weight I felt from those words as my dad spoke. The words hung in the air for a moment *"...Who greatly loves all of us."*

I repeat the words often enough in worship songs. *He loves me. Oh, how He loves me.* I skim through devotionals as they repeat the words over and over. But they don't sink in. *Oh, how He loves me.*

I don't remember the times when I didn't know He loved me. So I forget what it was like, the not knowing. Then I lose track of how I came to know that He loves me at all. How do I know He loves me? I became familiar with the sentence, but I had forgotten the meaning. I didn't seem to understand the context anymore.

The word "chagrin" is a classic example of this. I have a prolific (large) vocabulary. I enjoy using words that dance off my tongue. Therefore, I got into the habit of using the word 'chagrin' because I think it's a fun word to read, write and say.

I would use 'chagrin' to communicate a wry sense of amusement. I used chagrin in that context over and over and over until someone stopped me to ask what it meant. Much to my "chagrin," I looked up the definition to find it meant something completely different than what I thought: "Distress or embarrassment at having failed or been humiliated."

Don't worry; the irony was not lost on me.

Now think about how a similar error of misunderstood context could affect faith. Not only can a misuse of the character of God in conversation affect others, but a proper understanding of Him is vital for the believer. It informs everything we do.

Who can argue that someone's belief about how the planet was created won't color their perception of the life we live on it? Moreover, can anyone say our lives are not defined by who we believe is in control of it?

Our lives are a daily testimony to whatever it is we put our ultimate faith in. Do we put our trust in God? Or do we believe we are left to ourselves?

If I say with my mouth that I believe in God, and that He holds the Earth in His hands and that He loves me, my actions should be similarly informed. If I trust in that as the foundation of my reality, others will be able to observe me trusting in that truth. I may feel fear, but I will not live there. I will live victoriously because of what I know to be true.

My life can be a testimony to the daily remembering of His faithfulness; I only have to remember it.

DEVIL'S ADVOCATE

One of my favorite challenges to my faith wasn't a question about God or Jesus or the church. It ultimately was a question about God, because it was a question of His character. Let me tell you about it.

I had no warning. My friend and I were in the middle of eating breakfast at a local diner. Her brow slowly furrowed, as if she could fill the growing silence of our conversation with facial expressions.

"You see...what I don't get..." she sighed. "How do you know that the devil..." she paused as she violently stabbed her eggs with her fork. "How do you know that the devil wasn't looking out for Adam and Eve? I mean, how do you know that God wasn't cruel? How are you so sure that the devil was lying?" She paused again, tilting her head like a confused child. She didn't mean the question as a challenge. She genuinely wondered how I knew.

Honestly, now that she was asking, I was wondering that myself.

I mean, I knew.

I *knew* that I knew.

But how did I know?

See? The question comes up a lot.

I thought back to Rose and the problem of the missing 110. I always remember this story whenever someone asks me a question both simple and hard. "This should be basic," I always think. And it is, but it also isn't.

I find it odd that we can have peace with the fact that there are fundamentals of science that most people don't entirely understand, yet we struggle to admit the same can be true in our faith.

If we aren't frustrated by the fact that we don't immediately understand the universe at a molecular level, I think it also stands to reason that we shouldn't be frustrated by not understanding our faith on a molecular level. We can indulge momentary frustration if it fuels us into deeper understanding; choosing to ignore that lack of knowledge is dangerous.

When did I forget that realizing there is something I do not know is an invitation to learn more? When I was in school, I got excited when I encountered a new concept. I never felt ashamed if I didn't know the answer to something I hadn't learned yet—it became an adventure to find the new facts and know them for myself.

I can't tell you why it took me so long to apply this concept to my faith, but I can tell you my faith radically changed once I did. Once I had the proper view of the questions people would ask me about God, the more I grew excited to answer them.

To those who don't know who God is, dedication to Him can look puzzling. That confusion is understandable. It makes me feel awful about how I used to view them; I used to see those questions as an attack on my relationship with Him. Having more patience with my own lack of knowledge has given me patience with the misinformation of others. Now I see their questions as a request to be told about Him. It's a great perspective, and biased though I may be, I'm convinced that it's the right one.

Viewing questions as opportunities to learn has also shown me how much deeper my roots can still grow. *I'm not finished yet!* How awesome is that?

So, back to my friend's question. *How do I know?*

"I know," I eventually responded, "because I know his character."

I know Who we are talking about. No, I wasn't with Adam and Eve when they were tempted in the garden, but I have heard the same insidious whisper, "Did God really say...?"

I've known temptation, and I know who fuels it.

The devil has told me those lies. I've wrestled with the thought that God is somehow holding out on me. I've entertained the idea that I'm not clean enough to deserve the love of the Father.

That said, I know the truth of the Father's love. I have witnessed the grace of God as one whom the Lord has seen fit to redeem. My heavenly Father takes every ugly thought, every deceitful whisper and every heart-breaking accusation and throws them out into the night. He wore the weight of these lies and my sin so that I could live free from them for eternity. He replaces each claustrophobic lie with whispers of his own:

You don't earn love; I give it to you freely.

You don't earn value; I have already proven you are of great value.

You are not in danger of losing anything that I have promised you.

I can't comment on the green of the leaves of the garden nor the weight of the apple, yet I stand on trial for truth, a character witness of both the perpetrator and the Redeemer.

I know who both of them are because I have experienced them.

I know who they have proven to be to me.

Who do you say that He is?

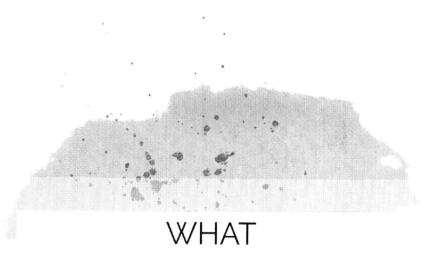

WHAT

I almost skipped writing this chapter.

My defense follows:

It was the October of 2016. Eighteen months beforehand, I suddenly realized I had written a book on accident. Blogs and essays written over the course of four years had a common theme, and they could be connected to form one rather consistent book.

Spoiler: you are holding that book.

I was in the middle of piecing together the sections, like taping together bits of a torn letter, when I had another realization:

"Shoot. I don't have a 'what.'"

I was markedly less enthusiastic about this realization. I was perturbed.

'What are we talking about?' It seemed stupidly simple. We were talking about faith—duh. We were talking about Jesus.

The annoyance was much like that in the nose-pinching pride of my dining room debate with Rose all those years ago. My motivation wasn't much different, either.

I was going to skip the 'what' in a book about the "who, what, when, where and why" of faith because I thought a reader could survive without it. I rationalized the audience of this book would likely be Christian and therefore would already know the what. So why bother?

I wanted a litany of valid reasons to write this chapter: reasons why someone would read a book about the 'what' of a subject without knowing it (for instance, learning).

Instead, I received an unnerving whisper to my soul.

I didn't feel disturbed or threatened. This whisper is frequent in my life. I find it unsettling because it always asks me to leave my comfort. The whisper of the I AM is constantly inviting me to something greater.

The whisper nudged, "Do you know '*what?*'"

Though the nudge corrects, it never condemns. The Father doesn't work like that. It was a gentle reminder, a nudge that said, "Daughter, I know that you know this. But do you remember it?"

It's like what I told you about the word chagrin: even though I used it in many conversations, I didn't know its true meaning, and even though I knew I was using it in the correct context, after years of use, I had forgotten how to explain it.

In the case of knowing the meaning of the word 'chagrin,' I looked it up on my phone. When it came to finding the 'what' of faith while I was in the middle of trying to write about it, I wound up at a loss for what to do.

So I gave up.

I mean, I didn't give up *writing*. This book proves I didn't surrender. However, I gave up pretending I knew 'what.' I couldn't even tell you if it was a "Here is what I know," or "This is what I live for," type of question. In my confusion, I took a cue from my friend in the conversation about chagrin.

I didn't know, so I asked.

Feeling childish, I offered up a silent prayer, "I don't remember 'what.' I should know 'what' I'm writing about, and I could use a reminder. Help a sister out. "

Instead of getting an answer, I got a quick jolt to my hip. I pulled my phone out of my pocket, horrified to notice the time. I was going to be fifteen minutes late to meet a friend for coffee.

I fired off a quick text apologizing for my tardiness before dashing over to our usual coffee shop.

Seventeen minutes later, I blustered in the front door, flustered and distracted. A corner of my mind still gnawed on the idea of 'what.' Another part of my brain was busy tabulating the rest of my day. The conversation of 'what' had been unscheduled, and my tardiness for this meeting meant that I was either going to be late for an evening service at church or I would miss the service altogether.

Hailey was blissfully unaware of my inner turmoil. She waved off my tardiness with her usual grace. Settling back into the overstuffed leather couch, Hailey began to update me on her life. The last time we had met she had been writing her first wedding ceremony. Since then, she had officiated the wedding and was full of witty recollections of the event. I laughed when pauses deemed it was appropriate. My mind still gnawed upon the question of "what."

*How can I not know **what**? Should I even be writing this thing?*

Hailey's hand suddenly slammed onto the couch between us, jolting me into focus.

"ANNIS." She now used the couch-slapping hand to support her head as she leaned into the story and said, "I meant to talk with you about this weeks ago, but it didn't seem like a conversation to have over text."

"Do tell." I smiled, sipping my coffee. Hailey was offering a new puzzle, and I enjoyed it far more than the one that was preoccupying me. What could possibly not be a text conversation for a pair of millennials?

"Well, I've been reading the devotions, as you suggested, and we just finished Mark. Well, Annis. No one ever told me that Jesus was sassy!"

I don't think I would have been more surprised if I woke up with my hair stapled to my bedroom carpet.

I'll explain:

Hailey and I met when Ms. Schmidt, our choir director, gave us the task of sharing a folder. A year apart, we were both performing as second sopranos for the high school's audition chamber choir.

Hailey and I quickly began a steady rhythm of whispered conversation and favored Disney lines in the ten-minute-long stretches when Ms. Schmidt's focus would be on another section of the group. Those first tentative conversations quickly flourished into late night meet-ups at the local diner.

There were many great things about our local haunt; one, it's open all 24 hours of the day! Another fantastic thing is the staff have no problem with guests wasting hours and hours in their booths, just as long as they paid.

As such, the diner was a hot spot for many high school students, whether as patrons or employees. In Hailey's case, she was both.

I would often slide into a booth as her shift was ending, ready to continue our discussions. Quickly exhausting the topics of our musical preferences and random Disney trivia, our interactions began to find their way to faith. With faith, we shared a thirst for knowledge, wide-eyed curiosity and little else.

Hailey seemed to find my Christianity refreshing. Despite being a third generation believer, my life and childhood had been one where I could either take hold on the anchor of Christ or I could get swept away. Having had my faith tested from a young age, I was also more comfortable than most with Hailey openly questioning it.

Hailey's life included some years in parochial school followed by a quick slide into paganism. The slide had begun as an act of teenage rebellion and then stuck. The years being tutored by nuns made her confident in her dismissal. "My people aren't His people," she would say, sipping at her water.

In hindsight, I'm surprised I didn't debate that point with her. For one, I love to argue. Secondly, what about me? I was one of their mutual people, right? However, I didn't say a word. I just kept being one of Hailey's people. She seemed so set in her ways that it didn't occur to me to try to be anything else. I just kept loving Hailey (incredibly easy) and listening to her (also easy—that woman knows how to tell a story).

I didn't ask about the particulars of rituals or spells, and she rarely asked about Bible stories or for descriptions of worship at my church. We talked about our people. We asked each other about our respective lenses toward the world and discussed how they affected our views on suffering, the afterlife, on abortions, homosexuality or prayer.

My favorite thing was when she would stump me. Hailey would ask a question, and I would realize it had never occurred to me. I would jot it down and research it, sharing my findings the next time we met. I loved how Hailey wanted to know these things, and I loved how her curiosity brought me into a deeper faith. Hailey wanted to know what I knew, and our conversations kept me in the habit of knowing how I knew.

Now and then she would look at me from across a table and say, "You know, you could make a good Wiccan."

Twice I replied, saying, "You know, I think you would really love Jesus."

"Nah." She would wave the comment off, "We've met, and we don't go to the same parties."

I would smirk, and sit in what she probably thought was silence.

I prayed.

From the moment we opened our shared folder in high school, I felt a deep desire to pray for Hailey. My prayers were simple, and they were always the same: *Jesus, let Hailey see who you are, not who the world makes you out to be.*

It felt odd how much I enjoyed praying for Hailey. One Saturday night about six years into our friendship, a conviction hit me from out of left field. I was halfway down the stairs with a laundry basket full of clothes when I suddenly needed to sit down, struck with a very simple instruction.

"Pray for Hailey. Pray for Oren. Pray for them right now."

Hailey's son Oren had been in the NICU since his birth the November before. He was born at 26 weeks due to Oligohydramnios, which is a fancy Greek way of saying that he didn't have enough mniotic fluid to survive in the womb.

I had visited in February, and with winter germs I had decided to keep in text contact with his proud mama until he was safely home. By all accounts, things were looking good. His care staff had begun to discuss when Oren might be released to go home. It made no sense for me to pray for them; to my understanding, there could not possibly be a need.

But this compulsion would not be denied. I was to pray, and I was to pray *now.*

So I sat on those stairs and prayed. Ten minutes later, I felt the Lord instructing me, "Text Hailey. Tell her that you are praying for her and Oren."

"God, really?!" I thought. "I'm going to look crazy—there is no reason for me to be texting her right now."

The only answer was a gentle repeating, "Text Hailey and tell her you are praying for her."

So I did. When I look back on the moment, I wish I would have called. But I wasn't told to call Hailey; I was prompted to text her. I plugged away on my flip phone, T9 turning my typed numbers into words. Within fifteen minutes I received a cheery response back, "Thank you, Annis! It means so much that you pray for us. I appreciate it!"

I read her text, thinking, "Well. That was nice, I guess, but it seems like it was kind of unnecessary." I shrugged. I picked up my basket and continued with my tasks, continuing to pray throughout the evening.

The next morning, the sun rose and so did I. I began the wearied hum of starting my day, turning the coffee on for the household. I plugged in my laptop and wiped the sleep from my eyes. The morning felt studied and routine. Little did I know the sun had risen on a different world.

I opened my Facebook. It felt like ice dropped down my spine.

"My baby fought as long and as hard as he could..."

Throughout the night, Oren had died.

I stared at the screen. Tears pricked at my eyes. The tip of my nose seemed to go numb. My fingertips felt disconnected from my body as I typed out my condolences.

How could this be?

There was a hum in my ears like jet engines after takeoff. My mind filled with static. It lingered for weeks, like a haze. I went to Oren's life celebration, only to slip out early. I would later carry a deep shame that, in my immaturity, I had excused my departure with a quick, "I can't do this," to the stoic and forgiving face of my dear friend. Somewhere between that regret and grief, Hailey and I quietly fell out of contact.

Five years passed with well-wishes extended on our respective birthdays and little else. The distance did nothing to stop the desire to pray for Hailey. In fact, the desire only grew. I would hear the whisper in my heart to pray for Hailey at least once every other week, God's faithful invitation into being part of getting His will done.

"God, even if I only get to see a Facebook post of her knowing You," I'd pray. "I just pray she knows You. I pray she knows You. I want her reunited with Oren in Heaven. I pray that she learns You have invited her to the party."

It is to Oren's credit that I continued. Oren taught me prayer is never fruitless.

Then came 2016, and with the New Year came a changing tide. I began attending a new church, where I began serving on the setup team. A week or so into my assignment, my friend Des and I realized we had a mutual friend—guess who? Hailey. Hailey sat next to Des at work. We quickly took a "What a small world!" selfie and sent it to Hailey, to which she responded, "You go to church together?! I should join you sometime!"

A month passed, and I got another notification. This time Hailey was inviting me to Sisterhood Night, a quarterly women's event at MY church. It was so ludicrous I laughed out loud as I quickly changed my plans to attend the event with her. Over yogurt parfaits and sparkling water, we caught up on our lives. When I recalled that the last time we had seen each other was Oren's memorial, Hailey declared that was five years ago and therefore far too long. After worship, she asked if I knew any of the songs that we had sung. I gamely listed the songs that I knew and gave her more recommendations. As we walked to our cars, since Hailey wasn't much of a hugger, we waved goodbye to each other from across a parking spot before going our separate ways.

I thought that was the end of that. I thought things would continue much as they always had.

Delightfully, my assumptions have a tendency to be wrong.

Three months passed and it was time for the second Sisterhood Night of the year. This time, we decided to meet up for dinner beforehand. The location wasn't a question. We met at our usual place, agreeing to carpool after we ate. She plugged her phone into the stereo system as I hopped into her car.

"I made a church jams playlist," she crowed. "Sing along!"

My eyes nearly bugged out of my head.

My friend, we jammed. We harmonized to Hailey's church jams playlist as she drove us to Sisterhood Night. I got out of the car to check if her "Wiccan Clergy" bumper sticker was still on her car's rear windshield. Yup, it was!

My prayers that night were delighted but bewildered. "Jesus, I don't know what you are doing, but please keep showing up!"

Friendly reminder: if you invite Jesus to the party, He will always make an appearance. This time was no exception.

The next day I opened my computer to another Hailey post. This time, she made a good-humored joke about an alternate name for Bible studies: "Why is Bible Study not called The Good Book Club?" I started my comment saying how great of an idea I thought that was. Suddenly I found myself typing, "If I started one, would you come?"

I have had many moments when I have been surprised with my own daring, but I think that particular moment will forever be a favorite.

The courage paid off, and she accepted.

"Totally!"

When I offered her a Bible she could use for the study, she politely refused. She explained that she had already researched which translation would be best for a newcomer to start with and thus informed, purchased one that she could color in. My incredulous prayers continued as I introduced her to my church's daily Bible reading plan.

Which brings our story back to the moment Hailey realized Jesus is sassy. It was also the moment I realized Hailey had been more faithful to complete the daily readings than I had.

Eleven years, echoed through my brain. ***Eleven*** *years.*

"All those years of Catholic school, and did anyone tell me that Jesus was sassy? Like, *guys*. That was a little bit of necessary information."

No one had ever told her what exactly Jesus was saying.

Hailey had no idea who Jesus was until now.

I sat, stunned as Hailey continued listing her recent revelations. After learning Jesus was sassy, she had been stunned to learn that Jesus was only in four books of the Bible.

She declared, "I thought He was the main character!"

I was also stunned to realize she hadn't known before. Like our diner dates of old, Hailey brought my attention to something that had never occurred to me.

I shook myself out of my stupor, finally asking her what caused her to realize Jesus was sassy.

She considered it for a moment. "I don't know," she mused. "I think it was in Mark. Jesus had just fed the 5,000, and then immediately afterward He needed to feed people again, and everybody worried. His response was just, 'You guys. Have you not been paying attention?'"

She sighed. "And it's like, poor disciples! I get you!" She sipped her coffee. "I mean, obviously I haven't been paying attention. I didn't even realize who Jesus was. Who knew that He is someone I would actually want to talk with! If I didn't know that, what else don't I know?

"I mean, do I even know what it means to be a Christian?"

The gnawing over the concept of 'what' stopped the moment Hailey asked about it.

"Well," I paused, trying to steady myself. "I can't speak for everyone, but I could tell you what it means to me?"

She nodded. I opened my mouth, and this is what came out:

"For me, I'm saved through Jesus. It is no small, everyday thing. He saved me from death. Jesus saw me in the depths of my sin and loved me there and then. He loved me enough not to leave me there. He took action, dying on the cross to pay the debt of my sin. Once I accepted Him, I received salvation and a relationship with Him.

What it means for me to be a Christian in my everyday life is that I am aware that my Savior also died for every person I meet and interact with. He loves these people, He cherishes them and He desires a relationship with them. The more I follow Him, the more I have His heart for other people. I'm not always perfect at it, and every day I get to improve. I get to be a representative of Christ. I get to carry the love that saved me, and I get to share it with the people I meet. I get to cherish them. Sometimes I get the chance to tell them.

It is a life that I love."

By the time I finished, I was crying. I didn't know why. Hailey was crying, too, and she said it was my fault for making her cry.

We smiled at each other in silence.

My spirit was still. My striving ceased.

Hailey looked at the clock and asked, "What time does the evening service start?"

I laughed shortly, "6 o'clock."

"But Annis!" She went to show me her phone. *6:05 pm.* I shook my head.

"I know, Hailey," I said. The clock on the wall also read 6:05. "You are worth it."

She shook her finger at me. "Don't you make me cry again!"

Don't get me wrong; I still forget the "what" of my life sometimes. I forget that Jesus is the most exciting thing that will ever happen to me. I get distracted or caught up in my striving and desires rather than in what God is doing in a given moment. I'm glad for the wrestling I had that day, though. I marinated on "what" for two hours before Hailey asked me about it. What came out of my mouth was the purest reflection of my faith I've ever shared. It had a lot less to do with what I was saved from and was almost entirely about the love He gives me to share and the life I live because of Him.

Speaking of the life I live now; it's kind of cool.

I started editing this chapter six weeks after we discussed the sassiness of Christ. I was late (again) to meet Hailey at the same coffee shop. Again, we discussed our lives and exchanged opinions on faith. Then we opened our laptops, each of us writing the different things we were learning from the same sassy Jesus.

Little had changed, but one big thing had: Hailey had finally opened her invite to the party. As I put my final edits on the chapter three months later, Hailey and I are currently leading a lifegroup together.

If someone had told me this was going to happen, I would have laughed. Hailey and I have been discussing how many people in the Bible laughed, so I know I'm not alone in consistently being floored by the ridiculous extravagance of God.

In short, life is kind of cool when you are focused on knowing what you know and what you're living for. Some might not think it's all that revolutionary, but we all need the reminder.

Or at least, I obviously did. I hope it helped you, too.

WHEN

ANNIS WOULD

AMSTERDAM, THE NETHERLANDS

I am sitting at a small cafe table, and it is the picture of a perfect European evening. The breeze off the canal is unseasonably warm for late March, and my coat is hanging from the back of my chair. I lean into the old wood, my fork dancing across my plate. The gentle screech of metal fills the silence for me as I think.

My friend Leonie waits patiently, taking another bite of her Dutch apple pie. We sit, eating our pie, both having arrived in Amsterdam within hours of each other. I'm here exploring with my friend, Zelphia. Leonie came from Germany for a dance audition that had gone poorly. I'm American. She is German. Even with her near-fluent English, we have a translation barrier that requires some consideration.

Not to mention her question.

"When did you know that you wanted Christ?"

It wasn't an unexpected question, necessarily. We were staying at a Christian hostel, and Zelphia and I had told Leonie we had met in a church ministry.

Now I was caught in the mental acrobatic act of trying to come up with the words to explain my testimony in a way that would be easy for Leonie to translate and understand. I usually try to be more prepared. I smiled, remembering the first time I had heard the word 'testimony.' I had been 20 years old and at a new church where this new word was thrown around like a baseball. *What's your testimony? This is my testimony.*

I remember thinking, "I don't know what a testimony is, but I'm pretty sure I don't have one." I sat silently in many Bible studies, hoping they would skip me. *Should I have a testimony? Did I?*

I found the courage to ask a friend over dishes. Joel had been raised in this church, but he had an approachability the others didn't. Fellow foodies and sarcasm enthusiasts, we found ourselves in the same circle more often than not.

It's funny, now, to think of Joel as approachable when he was so combative. I would come up with an opinion based on emotions and feel-good theology only for him to burst my balloon with, "Tell me the Bible verse that backs that up."

What began as a frustrating conflict quickly became a fencing match of wits and Scripture that I delighted in. As I would research to see if there were Bible verses that substantiated my opinions, I quickly developed a love of Scripture that took root in me. The Word of God became a sword, alive and active in my hands as Hebrews 4:12 had promised.

As Joel was constantly questioning me, I knew he wouldn't mind if I asked a question of my own.

Joel's charm and good manners often soothed the offense of his combative nature, and aforementioned good manners frequently found him doing the dishes at dinner parties. While conversation moved from the dining room into the living room he would pop into the kitchen to finish off dishes for the host.

On the night in question, I was the host, so I followed Joel into the kitchen to scrub one of the baking pans. I kept my eyes on the caramelized goo rather than on him. I tried to toss the question out casually.

"What do they mean?" I asked, scrubbing a corner with steel wool. "When they talk about testimony?"

He put the plate he was drying down on the counter next to him, turning to look at me.

Refusing to look at him, I continued, "How do I get one?"

Joel took the non-verbal cue and turned back to the sink to begin washing another plate.

"Just tell me your story." He swirled a washcloth through a glass. "Tell me your life."

It was a long conversation, outlasting the pile of dishes needing to be cleaned. Through my story wove the thread of Jesus's faithfulness, a common theme he pointed out as we still remained in the kitchen, sitting on separate counters.

"That," he pointed, "is your testimony."

While I am grateful for my education in 'testimony,' I like Leonie's phrasing a lot better. It drops the 'Christian-ese' and gets to the heart of the matter; all of life is stories, and Christian life is no exception. Every story starts somewhere.

Mine starts in a bathtub.

When I remember how this all began, I find it easier to remember it as the girl I was then. I'm young, a toddler with blonde, curly hair and chubby legs. My eyes are vibrant blue and full of curiosity.

First, I remember afternoon light. The sun is cracking through the windows, leaving slices of light cut by the shadow on the living room floor. I smile at my aunt, pulling myself over to the couch where she is sitting. The fabric was stiff against my hands as I pull myself to stand beside her legs.

She is singing to me.

"Jesus loves me, this I know..." she runs a hand through my hair, fingers caught in the tangle of curls. I coo, doing my best to babble along with her. She picks me up into her lap as she finishes "...the Bible tells me so."

She hugs me close, and I feel no fear.

"It's true, sweet girl. It's true. Jesus loves you. Jesus loves you, and He is so big. He is so strong. Jesus will never leave you alone."

Another kiss to my forehead before she rests her cheek there.

"You ever feel alone, or scared, you call to Him. He'll be there."

A tighter squeeze.

"I promise, sweet girl."

Time passes, and I'm in the arms of a different woman. We're in a bathroom. I am in the tub, and she towers above me. I feel fear.

Of all the people I could share this story with, I wish I could go back and whisper it into my own ear. I wish I could hold my shaking hand, pull my toddler body from that bathtub and whisper the beautiful future to come into her small little ear. I wish I could tell her at this moment where it brings her.

However, this is a memory, and memories are no place for wishes. They are a place for remembering. So I do.

I remember my bones shaking, my lungs heaving and my own silent screams.

I'm too young to know the words that go with what I feel at the moment, but in the time that has passed, I have learned them. In the coming years I understand that I feel betrayed. Even at my young age, I know this woman, she is my mother, was supposed to protect me. I feel so afraid. Here she is, holding me down to slice my legs with a razor blade. Nothing about this feels right.

Every time I remember this, I am struck by how small I am. I feel defenseless. I remember my feeble attempts to fight.

I also remember giving up.

My vision goes slack and unfocused. I tried so hard to remember something good.

I'm too young to know the words for it, but I search for an anchor. Flashes of memory flit through my mind like gentle fire. I return to the sunlit family room in Ohio. I'm looking up into my aunt—my Tee Tee's face—and she is singing again.

Jesus will never leave you alone.

Red begins to join the water around my legs.

If you are alone, or scared, call out for Him. He'll be there.

Red begins to swirl around the drain.

I promise.

I don't know the words, but my young heart pleads. I feel empty. I feel alone. I feel weak. My mind forms the images, and they have a feeble weight. I call for Jesus to come. I whisper for His attention. I ask if He'll fill me. My plea is in tune with my heartbeat. I want you, Jesus.

He comes.

The songs are all accurate. God comes like a rushing wind, like an avalanche in both the feeling and sound. His power roars in my ears, and suddenly I am covered with a weight that I cannot name. Peace, a comfort, silence. Those words come close.

He is inside me, within my bones, and I overflow.

I have yet to learn words to describe what I felt then, and I suppose that is right. The closest translation, after much simplification, would be:

"Yes. I do."

It didn't stop the cuts from coming. It didn't halt the blood from joining the bathwater. It didn't numb the pain or the betrayal, but it anchored me. It buoyed me to survive.

If I could whisper in my tiny ear, I would tell little Annis what happens in the next twelve years.

My father, eventually, after an arduous battle, won sole custody of me. To my knowledge, he was the second dad in the state of Minnesota to do so. Despite my impulsiveness, aggression, selfishness and the nearly a dozen school suspensions I accumulated before sixth grade, he still wanted me. The value he held for me both baffled and angered me.

I regularly tested his resolve with tantrums. I did my best to push him and everyone else away before they could leave me. Despite the presence of Christ, I decided that I could protect myself. I refused to ever let myself be betrayed or abandoned again.

Childhood photographs show a transition from bright, lively eyes to both guarded and trapped. My smile was often forced as I began to comprehend what had happened.

All through this, I remembered. I knew without a doubt there was a God. I knew with each breath that He loved me. However, I became convinced that Jesus only loved me because He had to. You see, if He didn't love me, then He couldn't claim to love everyone.

My doubt did not stop Him from pursuing me. Still, He called to me. It burned me.

I eventually began to control my triggers and outbursts. It was less of a spiritual intervention and more understanding that I would end up in juvenile detention if I didn't. I improved because I am a creature of self-preservation. My self-value remained unchanged.

By middle school, I was declared to be 'functional.' By the time I was a sophomore in high school, I was relatively neutral in action. While I stopped ripping people's hair out and the principal didn't even know my name, it isn't as if I was good.

Ben is an excellent example of this. I was never cruel to him, but I also never extended the kindness I knew I should. We had been in the same circle of friends for over two years before a sour end to a relationship also ended our connection. I didn't speak up to defend him as friends spoke ill of him. Instead, I pretended not to see him when he would wave from across a crowded hall.

I didn't join in the conversation. I pacified myself. I would also comfort myself with the thought, "T*he halls are so crowded; there is no way he saw that I saw him."*

I was fifteen and I spent a lot of my time doing things I had no business doing. One of those things was going out trick-or-treating.

So Halloween came around, and that same group of friends went out, listing their complaints about Ben's character as we went from house to house. I kept feeling a nudge in my side. *Change the subject. You don't even have to correct them, just change the subject.*

I heard the call of something greater, and I ignored it. It was very easy to do.

November 1, 2004, was a school day. A sophomore, I walked to my first-hour class and sat outside the locked door. I doodled in my notebook, looking up when I heard the squeak of tennis shoes coming down the ramp.

There came Danny, dressed entirely in black (as usual) and looking downtrodden (more than usual).

"So...um...did you hear about Ben?"

I shook my head no, bewildered. *What could I possibly need to be told about Ben?*

Ben, too, was out trick-or-treating the night before with his best friend, who crossed a major highway in our town. At 17 years old, Ben boldly followed, despite crossing against the light.

The first driver swerved and missed him.

The second driver hit him and the brakes at the same time.

Through a series of circumstances that can shortly be summarized as the handiwork of God, I attended his wake. I talked to his mother, who passionately told me she was sure, given the appropriate time, that Ben and I would have been close. I told her I agreed, we were cut from similar cloth, but I was not brave enough to admit that the distance was my fault alone.

I walked up to Ben's coffin to look down at his lifeless form. I felt the presence of the Lord just as vibrantly as I did in the bathtub. Another avalanche overtook me, but it was not peace. It was not the comfort of before.

The only similarity was that I could not escape the weight of it.

It is only a sigh, heavy with sorrow. *"Who **are** you?"*

The question shakes my bones. It's Him, I knew that God is speaking; God asked a question I did not have an answer for.

In that moment, I wasn't sure that I knew who I was. I faintly realized that I had been living as an echo, repeating the choices of the people I was closest to.

I am not who I am supposed to be.

I inhaled deeply, my breath shaky.

Who am I supposed to be?

Again, He answered. With a rush, my mind was flooded with God's design for me. I was blown away by these images of an incredible woman. She laughed, she loved, she cared so deeply for other people. She cared about them before herself. She laid her life down. She served, and she did so with joy. She never counted the cost of loving because she knew Christ had already paid it.

The woman was beautiful, and God thought that she was me.

A million thoughts rose to fight the notion that I could ever be something so good.

There has to be some mistake.

I'm too selfish.

I'm too violent.

I'm too broken.

I can't. I just can't.

I don't even know where to start.

It's a funny thing, though, to see who you can be. Afterward, you just can't be who you are anymore.

I knew I couldn't keep living the way I was, yet I wrestled to find a way to get where I was apparently supposed to be. After two weeks of wrestling, I decide there must be only one option.

I gathered up the tools necessary to ensure that November 18, 2004, would be the last day of my life.

Spoiler alert: it wasn't.

The night of November 17, 2004, began with a fight with my dad. In the middle of our argument, I noticed how distraught he was. I suddenly realized he had been the one taking all of those childhood photographs. He had been the one on his knees praying for twelve years. He was the one who drove me back and forth to all of the different specialists, therapists and doctors...yet, I was still trapped.

He couldn't save me. I couldn't bear it.

The words flew out of my mouth before I could catch them. "Hey, well, don't worry. Soon you'll get to have the life you want. Tomorrow you're coming home to a corpse."

Thank God, he took me seriously. After losing his mother to suicide when he was 16 years old, my dad had pledged to listen and be an advocate for anyone who might be struggling. After a few phone calls, he told me to pack for the hospital.

I fought him at first. I had been pretty heart-set on a one-way ticket off the planet. Eventually, though, I packed my bags. Out of my hundreds of books, I picked only one.

My dad looked at the Bible in my hands, smiling sadly. "You know that you aren't being grounded, right? You're getting help."

Growing up, it was near impossible for my father to adequately punish me. Grounding me from television or radio only caused me delight since I loved time alone with my books. So he had taken up the practice of grounding me from my books; whenever I would need correcting, he would remove every book from my room except for one.

The same worn Bible that now rested in my hands.

I nodded, "I know. But I've read all those other books, Dad." I looked down at the book in my hands. "I think this might be the only one that can help."

We stood in silence for a moment. Then he said the words that changed my life.

"You should read Romans." He turned to get the car, keys jingling in his hands. "I think it helped my mom stay as long for as she did."

And so I did. Not that night—it was nearly 2:00 am by the time I got checked into my room at the hospital. However, the next day I read the entire book of Romans five times. I read it over and over each of the six days I was committed, and I became committed to what it began doing to me.

It slowly dawned on me: God knows you can't do this by yourself.

And that was never what I had been asked to do. I realized the real thing He was asking for was something I already wanted to do: surrender my life. The only difference was instead of dying, I would be transformed. Romans hummed with a promise: *You are going to be renewed.* In surrender, God would work to cultivate the beauty He had already sown.

He was eager to do this. He was eager because He loves me. Not as a completionist, not to save the world as a whole, but He loves me. He eagerly awaited my birth and sought me out through each of my days. He never left me alone.

Again, I remembered my desperate prayer in the bathtub . *I want you. My soul needs you.*

He who promised has been faithful. It has been over 10 years since those six days. The years between that day and my present are not easy ones, but they are years and moments in which Jesus was proven true. It did not magically get better. However, I would not trade or change one of the days since.

Because beauty came from all of it. Good came from it. My life became a beautiful thing, a testimony to the truth of Romans 8:28: "And we know that all things work to the good of those who love God and are called according to his purpose."

Each day is a re-remembering, a re-dedication, a new invitation. *I want You, Jesus. My life is dead without Your purpose. I want You.* The bathtub was my first, but each day after has been a new dedication, a new invitation. I need Jesus every single day, and I am so thankful that He has always answered my call.

Jesus has never left me alone.

I finish my story, both of our pies largely uneaten and cool on our plates. Leonie smiles from across the table. "Thank you for sharing your story," she says quietly. She takes a sip of her water, then asks, "Does Zelphia love Christ the same way you do?"

I'm taken aback for a moment. I think about each of the believers Leonie is encountering this weekend. Zelphia, the dozens of missionaries at the hostel, the seemingly random assignment of train seats and bunks for the night. We are a chorus of God's faithfulness, each one of us with a bright light and a different story. We sing with the same passion and key, but we all sing different songs. Our different testimonies sung in perfect harmony under the banner of Christ.

How can you tell them all? How can you explain it to someone who doesn't know?

"Zelphia loves Him with the same passion I do, but her story is different than mine. Everyone at the hostel—they love Him, too. I know they would love for you to ask."

We smile at each other once more and slip into comfortable silence. Our bill gets paid and we take off into the quiet Jordaan night. Our footsteps against the cobblestones join the sound of bike tires whirring past and the gentle whispers from many other cafes. Leonie shares stories about her childhood adventures in the forests of Germany.

I smile at the craziness of it all—that we are all such similar beings, separated by differences of mere chromosomes yet a myriad of distinct experiences.

I would love to know yours.

So tell me: *when did you know?*

WHERE

The evening air was thick with humidity. The dimly lit lounge off of University Avenue had a group almost on the verge of being a crowd, and a static whine filled the silence between Kayla and me. We sat in companionable silence as our friend's band ran through their last minute sound check before taking the stage.

It was July 2, 2015, moments before I turned 26. Marah and the Mainsail were about to make the headline performance for their CD release party. I expected nothing beyond the aforementioned good company and excellent music.

The night, however, had a mind of its own.

We have never determined what it was about the evening that jogged Kayla's memory, but we know that it did. Her eyes widened in surprise as she exclaimed, "I just remembered!" She pulled out her phone, and as she pulled open Facebook Messenger, I remembered as well.

A few weeks before, Kayla had returned from a short-term mission trip to Milan. Evergreen had grown into my church home, and Kayla and I had met when she began attending, as well. The church sent a small team of short-term missionaries to Italy over spring break each year. In 2015 there was enough interest to send two full teams back-to-back. Fully manned, the teams continued the long-standing tradition of offering English clubs on the University campus, separating the students based on their fluency level. Students would return daily for conversations with native English speakers to refine their skills. The students would then be invited to the team dinners and outings throughout the week. Building relationships as they built vocabulary, the entire church would pray for the opportunity to share the joy and love of Christ.

Kayla had especially connected with one girl, Natalie. They grew close throughout the week, and Kayla had left Italy with a new Facebook friend and prayer request. Four days later, Kayla had eagerly texted me.

"I'm going to need your words."

I had immediately responded, "Cucumber, medal, jabberwocky, shoe."

My cheekiness won me a stuck out tongue and a quick clarification: "Natalie asked me a question, and it's such a good one. First, I think you'll really enjoy it, but I also know that you will have better words for it. "

I had gamely agreed, and she had promised to show me the message the next time we hung out.

We hung out four different times before this night, but finally, we both remembered.

We huddled shoulder-to-shoulder around the high top table and poured over Natalie's message together.

One particular phrase caught my attention.

"I enjoyed having you here. Can I ask you a question? Where does your joy come from? The whole group had it, and it is so different. Is that normal for you?"

Is that normal for you?

It pings at something inside of me, waking a rogue sense of restlessness. I scrunched up my face as I began ripping pages out of the back of my planner, the desire to write becoming overwhelming.

I think back to my journey of faith, circling the pen on the paper to draw out the ink. In the same way, my memories begin to flow, bringing more story out of me.

I smile at Natalie's hesitation to ask a question. I consider how easy it is to assume that churchgoers don't comprehend doubt. I've often encountered the belief that those raised in the church are naive and don't know the questions that come from growing up outside of the faith.

I disagree. I would argue that faith is a series of even more queries.

I forget how old I was when questions nearly overwhelmed my belief. I must have been about 19, and my questions had become a flood of doubt. I wish I could say my faith went out with a blaze, or that there was any kind of passion as I left. But while that story is dramatic and engaging, it simply isn't true. I faded away from my church, drifting into a foggy kind of hate.

I had hated it because I missed it. What I had once felt joyfully burning within me was now vapors of smoke wafting around in my ribs.

I had been so confused. Surely I had lived enough? Hadn't God dug enough depth out of me to foster whatever else was needed? Time passed as I continued on my journey, alone. Slowly my bitter anger cooled into sadness, and in the breath of sobriety, my soul felt empty.

The emptiness left a lot of room for my shame to rattle around. I feel it's a common trait, not enjoying the fact that we are capable of doing the things we have done. There was one particular moment of sin that had an unnatural fondness for haunting me, and I would get paralyzed. I would do everything within my power to keep that offensive potential for depravity as far away from me as possible. It felt natural to assume that God did the same.

I had thought that while Christ had held my sin, He must have kept it at arm's length like a rotting carcass. I assumed the process was something like a dog owner dealing with a bird dragged in from the woods, saying, "Well, this is a thing you've done. I suppose I'll take care of it. It's not like we can keep it around."

Like a dog caught in shame, I put my tail between my legs. Then I fled. I ran from house church to Bible studies, trying to keep my feet two steps ahead of my shame. If I kept moving, maybe no one would be able to tell. I thought I could dupe Christ into thinking I was someone worth dying for.

Then I read something in 1 Peter 2: "He personally carried our sins in His body on the cross so that we can be dead to sin and live for what is right. By His wounds, you are healed."

In His body.

There was no hiding the shame from Him. He had consumed it. He saw into the very depths of me, taking the filth of my depravity from where I have stuffed it to the bottom of my ribcage...and then He took it.

He didn't just throw it away. Did you notice that?

He carries it within Himself. Christ took what I ran from and consumed the cancerous destruction it brought to my life so it would be nailed to the cross and die with Him.

Hebrews 12:2 describes Jesus as the author and finisher of our faith.

And why? Why did He do this? The verse continues, "Jesus, the author, and finisher of our faith, bore our sins for the joy set before Him."

That joy was a restored relationship. That joy was having a relationship with *me*. Even though He saw my worst, it was His joy to endure the cross. It was His joy to redeem me so that He could walk with me through questions, hardships and doubt.

Having written the life of faith, Jesus was not expecting my life to be one without questioning. No, the life of faith is one of questions and answers. They don't always come as quickly as we want them to, but as I grew more experienced in God's character, I became more accustomed to trusting Him in the wait.

As I mentioned, I wrote this letter in 2015. I would later dub 2015 my 'Job Year.' As I prepared to answer Natalie's question about where our joy comes from, I was in the middle of the worst year of my life.

God was in the midst of spending a year of trial and pain to get one sentence down to the core of my foundation. He whispered and exulted, "You are all that I say that you are."

In the middle of the upward march, I would get kind of sick of hearing that. I was tired of being reminded because I had forgotten exactly what it was He had said about me. I was too tired to remember.

I wonder if the weariness to remember is part of the reason the book of Job was written down first. The Bible was originally passed down in the oral tradition, but one of the first chronicles of faith put to paper was the story of Job.

The book starts with God, in Heaven, looking down upon the earth. In all of God's creation, Job's faith is what He delights in. He is a proud father, boasting in the accomplishments of a favored son. The devil overhears this, and challenges that the only reason Job trusts in God is because God has blessed him.

"Let me take something from him," he challenges, "and let's see how long his faith lasts. Let's see how long he praises You."

Despite the pain of seeing Job tried and questioning God's very character, God allows Job to be tested. He watches as Job's wealth, family and health are stripped from him until only God's delight in him remains. Forty-one chapters of gut-wrenching questions and foolish counsel culminate in an opportunity for Job to hash it out with the Lord. Hash it out he does. He beats his fists as he questions the Lord.

God, ever the gentleman, waits until Job is done and settled. Then God tells Job a few things about Himself.

Job ends his trials with one of my favorite verses on his lips:

"I HAD ONLY HEARD ABOUT YOU BEFORE, BUT NOW I HAVE SEEN YOU WITH MY OWN EYES."

JOB 42:5, NLT

My mind is blown every time I read this verse. God *Himself* stated this man had the greatest faith in all of the earth. Job is laying face down at the end of a significant trial. He is essentially saying that his previous faith—the greatest and most boast-worthy thing on the planet—was basically nothing compared to where the Lord had brought him.

God used the trial to make His most boast-worthy delight more splendid still. The thought had been a comfort in April as my heart was utterly broken by betrayal. A dear friend had shown romantic interest, but then I had learned I was not the only person he was pursuing. May had brought both a job transition as well as a bitter family dispute that threatened to sever relationships indefinitely. While portions of the family somehow became stronger, I was still waiting in the tension for complete restoration.

Even as I wrote to Natalie in early July, I was in the middle of the questions. More questions were coming before there would be answers.

However, I knew enough of Jesus to be confident in the answers Natalie was asking for.

In faith, I wrote this letter, and by faith, it was proven.

THE LETTER

Our friend Kayla told me that you have a question.

She did not forget about your question. She has been so excited about it, and she asked for my help in answering it. I hope you don't mind.

Despite oceans and mountains between us, we share the joy of knowing Kayla because she visited you in Milan. The two of you became friends while she was there with a team from our church. Over the course of two weeks, you met roughly thirty of my favorite people, and you noticed something worth asking about. Your question was this:

Can you tell me where your joy comes from? I'd like to talk about that when you get the chance.

Well, Natalie, the answer is yes. Yes, please. We can always talk about that.

The simple answer is this: we have joy because we are filled with more than ourselves.

Our thoughts and desires aren't only for ourselves. I don't mean that we aren't selfish or that we are good at thinking of other people's needs and feelings. Those are good things that become true of us as a result of the deep love of Christ, but they are not what fills us.

What fills us is love. True, secure love that comes from knowing the Creator of the universe desires us, pursues us and loves us as we are. Further, God accepts us as we are, but He also loves us too much to let us stay that way.

He knew our deepest secrets and the ugly mistakes we try to hide, and He still chose us. He paid a high price—death on the cross—that we might decide to accept the gift of His love and eternal life with Him. He did this for the joy set before Him, which the Bible says is us. We have joy because we are declared to be joy.

We are filled with the knowledge that He has that same desire and depth of love for each person we encounter. We get to carry His love for other people.

This might sound crazy coming from a Minnesotan girl who hasn't met you, but I hold the love of God for you! It fills me and delights me. It is an even greater joy to know that He brought one of my dearest friends across rivers, oceans and mountains so you could hopefully see what pure, Holy and glorious love looks like.

We have joy because we do not love as the world loves; we have joy because the love we have been given is a love that surpasses.

The world's love will disappoint. It turns to ashes in our hands. No one likes to admit it, but the world's love is not enough.

But this love, the love we carry for each other and for you—this love is different. This love never ends. This love is consuming. It overflows. It changes everything.

I would also love the chance to talk with you more. I really hope that you will write back because I honestly never get tired of talking about how much God loves us. How He loves us individually, uniquely, completely.

I am glad that in His great love He gave me the opportunity to write to you.

WHY

Let's be honest, "why" questions are rarely cute. They are deep, groaning questions, because "why" is an issue that is usually asking for an explanation for why something is the way that it is.

The "why" questions start popping up as soon as we can speak:

"Why do I have to brush my teeth?"

"Why do we wear clothes?"

"Why do we have to eat broccoli?"

I once worked with a man who genuinely admired children; he was a bit like Jesus in that way. He encouraged his colleagues to challenge him. He wanted each of us to ask him a child-like "why" when he proposed a new idea, and once he provided an answer for the first "why," he wanted us to ask four more "why" questions.

Children persist in asking why until they finally comprehend a concept. Somewhere in adulthood, I picked up the habit to stop asking "why" after about two questions. In the attempt of pursuing childlike faith, I started to wonder upon "why" questions with regularity.

I asked myself, *"Why did you stop asking why?"*

I didn't want to show my hand. I didn't want anyone around me to know that I wasn't sure of what was going on around me. I wanted to appear in control. I wanted to appear confident, even though I wasn't.

Why aren't you confident?

I'm not confident in my answer because I stopped asking. Instead of using the opportunity to learn more about the issue, I chose to ignore it to get other things done.

Why are you ignoring it?

I ignore the question because I don't want to admit that I don't understand. I want to be respected. I feel like asking the question "why" is acknowledging that I don't deserve authority in a situation. I like being in charge. I don't want to lose control over the situation I'm in.

Why do you want to be in charge?

Calling the shots makes me feel very grown up. I like having the answers, and I don't like feeling like I don't know them. If I lose the upper hand, it's because I have admitted that I don't know.

Why don't you know?

Ha. Well, I don't know because I stopped asking questions.

I cannot tell you how often I have stopped asking 'why' because I felt like the question on the tip of my tongue was one I should already have answered. I would silence my question out of shame and then mimic the actions of the person who knew the answer.

Ability to 'not know' is one of the many reasons I love my friend Todd.

Once, Todd and I were both in a season of waiting for answers. One evening, our Bible study had just ended, and other conversations were starting around the room. We asked each other how we were doing. Now, you should know, Todd is one of those rare individuals who actually wants to know. One of my favorite exchanges with him went as such:

"Hey, Annis! How is it going?"

"Oh, I'm good!" I smiled.

"Good. But how is it going?"

Everything about Todd invests into a conversation. When he is given any amount of someone else's time, he takes full advantage. He's fully present in the moment before him.

I didn't want to answer Todd's question. I had been chewing on a gross question for a while, and it was like trying to chew on a chunk of fat. It wouldn't dissolve.

Jesus, why am I still here?

I don't ask in a harmful way, just to be clear. That ship had sailed in November 2004. I also wasn't asking it for direction or asking for God to reveal my purpose. I was in a season of pretense. I masked my questions with lofty intentions, thinking that flowery words would make doubt feel more appetizing to talk about. My favorite mask to wear was saying that I asked 'why' out of homesickness for Heaven. "I was just dreaming of home, and wishing I had been there."

Sounds super holy, right? It would be awesome if it were true.

The reality was I asked out of childish obstinance. *Why are we still standing in this line at the grocery store? Why aren't we doing something more fun?* If I don't like where I am, I start to get impatient, and for the love of Himself, God better have a good reason for making me wait.

Not Todd, though. He has innocent joy and childlike faith. Todd is a fantastic leader because he is honest about the questions he is asking. I learned from his example that the leader who asks questions frees up the entire group to seek to understand rather than to follow blindly.

So as I was sitting there, angrily expressing myself and my dissatisfaction with the holding pattern I found myself in, I said, "I know that I'm going somewhere, I just don't know where. And honestly," I paused, beginning to liberally apply my faux-holiness, "I don't want to go from one holding pen to another. I just want to go home."

I said it with the understanding that no one can argue with a desire for Heaven. However, I also knew I was saying it as an escape hatch out of what God was calling me into.

Todd considered that statement for a moment. That's one of my favorite things about him; he never makes someone feel like their question was dumb.

"I can understand that," he nodded. "I've been asking a similar question."

Todd's childlike faith doesn't stop with the freedom to ask questions. His childlike faith fully extends to the expectation that his question is going to be answered.

"I've been trying to enjoy faith," he finished. "As I've realized that while there are many things we will have in Heaven, faith will not be one of them."

I sat there for a moment. My childish heart stopped in the midst of the temper tantrum. *What do you mean we won't have faith?!*

At that time, I felt like faith was the broccoli of our spiritual feast. I understood that God thought that by faith a lot of good things would happen to me. Often I would put it on my plate with the hope that God would give me blessings, the spiritual equivalent of fresh brownies for dessert.

"Annis had faith! Two helpings of blessings for her!"

At Todd's assertion, I suddenly questioned that mindset. His statement pinged something in my soul. Faith becoming a limited-time offer changed the game entirely.

He continued, "When we're in Heaven, we won't need to trust God to come through. He will be right there in front of us. All of God's promises will already be fulfilled, and we will only enjoy Him and enjoy them. We get to build our relationship with Him then by trusting Him when we can't see Him now." He smiled despite his circumstances, as Todd often did.

"I don't think we'll have deep regrets in Heaven, but I believe we'll be aware of opportunities we missed. As I've been asking about it, I've realized I don't want to see His face and think, 'You are so good. You told me that you were so good. I see now that it is true. I wish I had trusted You when I had the chance.'"

Todd is not the first person to say there are a few things we are given here that Heaven has no need of, but I often need reminding. Gifts trusted into our hands with the intention of being given to the people we pass.

I think of it like living in a world colored only in black and white and realizing there is vibrant color smashed onto my hands. We are here to smack the color onto as many things as we possibly can, forever "it" in a spiritual game of Tag, touching each person as we pass them with a smear of the breath of heaven. We pass it along, and instead of crying, "You're IT!" we cry out, "You are loved! You were created!"

We carry the color of Heaven to brighten the world and awaken it from the sin that has deadened our senses.

When I realized what Todd was saying, that faith has an expiration date, I suddenly remembered a night years before.

I had settled onto my pillow, settling my cheek against the cotton. I began to dream in the usual fashion. I closed my eyes, forgetting consciousness and the life on the other side of my eyelids, allowing my mind to believe fantastical things.

Forgetting that I lay in bed with my eyes closed, my brain instead decided that I was standing in the middle of a busy sidewalk, surrounded by people.

I immediately grinned, neck looking up to the skyscrapers stretching up before me. I adore cities. I love the bustle of them, the intersection of so many people's days into one small bit of asphalt.

I've been known to sit on bus benches or airport terminals, watching people make their way to their destinations. Often I'll sip on some coffee and let my mind boggle as I consider the fact that each person walking past me has a belly button. Each person once grew inside of a womb. I sit and recognize that each passerby had to learn how to walk, how to talk, to put on their pants and put a spoon into their mouth. I like to wonder if they comb their hair into the same style their grandmother used to, or if their father taught them to tie their shoes.

I do the same here, part of my brain still releasing reality and reminding me that I'm in a dream. I look at the phones of passers-by with abandon, reading texts and judging musical tastes.

As I observe, I begin to notice a common trend. As common as belly buttons (unseen), each person is wearing a thick rope necklace (very noticeable). The line is thick and corded, the width of two of my fingers pressed together.

Just as each person has eyes, ears and noses, an identically thick rope braid rests on each person's collarbone. My pointer finger traces along the length of my own, finding the weight of it comforting around my neck.

My fingers wander to the back of my neck. I feel the rope connect into a coiled knot, and then two roughly cut edges. I instantly looked to the necklaces around me and saw that while we all wore necklaces, not all of them were like mine.

Some have cut, frayed ends peeking out from under ponytails. Many others were still intact, defying gravity to extend up among the clouds. I push through the crowds, questions like fireworks in my mind.

I arrive at an intersection and look down each street; as far as the eye can see, lines fall from the heavens to connect with the necks of those passing by.

I am perplexed.

Someone knocks into me, jolting me out of my daze and knocking me off-balance. Stepping back to keep myself upright, my right hand grazes against my thigh, fingertip brushing cold metal. I look down to see an ornate dagger sheathed in worn leather, weathered with age. I undo the binding, holding it up to my eyes. Seeing my face reflected in it, my mind dings with a distant memory. The dagger had been a gift.

I return it to my holster, setting off for answers.

I continue to walk through the city, more oddities coming to my attention. Time stands still; the hands on old clock towers don't seem to move. The time displayed remains frozen. The sun stays at peak height, never moving further across the sky.

I also notice more and more cut tethers. We share a purposeful stride through the city, paired with an on-guard demeanor. The pace and slight crease to the brow set us apart in a crowd, and our eyes meet as we pass on staircases or strolls through the park. We will smile at each other and quickly nod a greeting in the other's direction; the lack of a rope strand is a brotherhood.

As a brotherhood, the untethered were interlopers among the tethered. They appear to live the same endless day; work, lunch breaks, walks through the park are the same to both the untethered and the tethered. People wave hello and they strike up casual conversations; there appears to be nothing to set us apart, except that some of the people have daggers and some people have leashes.

I slid through the city like water, stopping when I heard a blade being unsheathed. I turned my focus to the sound, feeling like my head was underwater. A man in his early twenties with a trimmed beard, wearing a worn black t-shirt, held his dagger in one hand. The wind rustles the trees above him. The woman across the table from him is in her forties, bright red lipstick, copper hair coiled in a chignon and a coral dress flapping around her knees as the breeze picked up.

I waited. Was he going to cut the rope for her?

No.

He placed the dagger on the table, sliding it across. Smiling.

She looked at it, tentatively reaching a manicured hand towards the knife. She pauses, looks up at her rope's line to the sky. She reaches her right hand back to feel it connect to the cord around her neck. Tugging on the line, she deliberates.

Her left hand reached to the dagger testing the weight of it in her hand.

I looked away before she chose.

Out of the corner of my eye, I noticed the clock tower. The clock hands that had once been frozen at half past the hour now showed the time as a quarter til the frozen hour. A clanging of church bells filled the air, and a gray fog slowly fell upon the city.

Unnerved, I turned away from the tower, walking down the street to the next corner.

As I waited for the light to change, an elbow knocked into mine. I turned to see a dear friend. The same smile I had seen across dozens of coffee shop tables, captured in countless photos of adventures, caught me in the sea of people. Her tether pulled roughly across my cheek as I pulled her into a hug.

I playfully tugged on it, smiling as I waved my dagger at her. We had this exchange many times before.

She returned the playful smile, shaking her head with a twinkle in her eye. *Not today. Maybe later.*

The signal switches to walk, and she waves as she crosses the street. Mirroring her, I wave as she slips into the throng of people, her rope dancing with her walk as she bobbles like an anchor.

I wait on the street corner as darkness seeps into the color of the sky. I lean against a building, looking at my watch out of habit. I don't recall the position of the clock hands as I watch as a familiar pair of shoes stops in front of mine.

I look up to the goofy grin of another dear friend. My mind fires off memories of bonfires, camping conferences, Bible studies and fireworks. Years have passed since those days, but youth has yet to leave him. Boyish enthusiasm still lights up his face, a jesting twinkle in his eye as he very pointedly sheathes his dagger. My eyes widen, and his answering smile just might rip his face apart.

He doesn't say it, and I don't have to ask. I know that look; someone borrowed his dagger.

I jump up to hug him and follow him as he walks down the street. He talks more with his hands than he does with words, and our joy nearly overwhelms the approaching darkness.

We walk, and I see him laugh, but I do not hear it leave his mouth. I feel like I'm walking in slow motion. From the corner of my eye, I see the clock tower again.

The clock hands are moving; they are recklessly circling the dial, the entire clock face wobbling with the force of them. Somewhere, somewhere, the tower is chiming 12 o'clock.

My mouth still smiles, but my deafness has become complete. I turn back to my friend as the ground slips out from under us. Like a trap door swinging on a hinge, the street suddenly becomes a slide, and we are dropped into the depths below.

There is no time to even think of clutching at asphalt as it roughs up my bare skin. It is a 10-foot drop that takes less than a heartbeat, and I find myself crashing into a waiting net. I roll, haphazardly knocking limbs against others who have fallen. I struggle to my hands and knees, looking around into a sea of familiar faces. They were not familiar necessarily because all of them were known, but rather because I feel the bewilderment on their faces mirrored on mine.

Somehow, we are all safe, and we are mystified.

The net is uneven, and I struggle to stand. I turn to ask my friend a question as a gasp cuts through the crowd. I take his hand to pull myself to my feet as every head turns to see one woman in the middle of the crowd.

The net slowly becomes solid ground beneath my feet. The fading light hits her face, slices of dark contrast falling upon her cheeks. Her hand covers her mouth, which is wide open in horror. Her eyes slowly close over a flooding of tears.

There is sorrow in the sky, just a swift drop above us.

I see others look up, their hands quickly covering their mouths. My ears feel stuffed again as I inhale deeply.

I don't want to look.

Somewhere, distantly, the bells are still chiming. I think an alarm clock somewhere is screaming.

I look at my watch; it's time for me to wake up.

My time is nearly done.

I look up.

I don't know what was expected, but I was not prepared for what I found. I lift my head, and my eyes are full of blue-gray skies fading into dusk, white clouds slowly giving way to gray.

The sight would almost be reasonable, if not for the shadows.

Little black shadows suspended, dancing in an errant breeze, sitting perfectly level like birds on a telephone wire.

In short, I looked up to see the bottoms of shoes.

I woke from that dream in a cold sweat, covered by a new kind of gravity. Some dreams are pizza, and there are some that I need to take time in prayer to wrestle with and discern. Not this one; I knew what this dream meant in an instant.

I wish I had trusted You when I had the chance.

Let's be honest; Christ died to save us and to be in perfect relationship with us. If the answer to my "why" were about me, I would have been returned to Heaven the moment I accepted Christ. God has done it before; He did it with Enoch, Elijah and also Jesus. God can do it.

I'm not here for me; I'm here for them.

I'm here because there are people who don't know yet. I'm here because there are hurting people, captured in sin and deprived of their heavenly value. There are thousands upon thousands of people unaware that a great King loved them so much that He gave His only Son to die for them. God knew their great sorrow and made a Way for them.

I'm here, planted in the path of the lost and wandering to call out the darkness. To cry, "Look, there is light. By it, we can see! By it we can live!"

In short, why am I here? I'm here because Christ is more than good; He is true.

I want to be, too.

CLOSING

My dear friend, that about wraps up our time together. I have so enjoyed it.

Life is a story, yes, but life is also a series of questions. I hope that now you feel more equipped to answer them.

I pray, if you are a believer, you were reminded of our Teacher. Remember we get to flip to the end of the book and see all of the questions already solved, all of our temptations and worries already conquered by our perfect, empathetic High Priest (Hebrews 4:15).

If you started this book with questions, I hope you know where to find their answers.

Whether you pick up or abandon the cross of Christ, I trust you leave this book feeling confident as to why.

I hope, after reading this book, you are a little surer of your answers. If you don't feel like you have the answers, I hope you are more confident in asking those questions.

In short, I hope this book was unlike anything you've read before. I pray it was a conversation, because I honestly have no desire to tell you what to think. I want you to feel equipped to know how to think for yourself.

Oswald Chambers once wrote, "When the truth is preached, the Spirit of God brings each person face to face with God Himself."

I hope you have found yourself face to face with God Himself. I pray you can remind yourself of the truth on a daily basis. I pray for your power, your peace and your journey home.

I hope, above all else, that I will see you there.

In short, I hope you know.

ACKNOWLEDGEMENTS

There are many people who made this book possible, and I am going to do my best to highlight the major players:

First, to Sammy, for lending me her computer and encouraging me to begin the real work of editing while the rest of my community was sleeping eight time zones away. Sammy, that visit was a miracle that changed my life in more ways than one. Thank you for inviting me.

Then we have Hailey. This book and my life would not be the same without her; Hailey, you have changed me for good.

To Jenna, our third amigo and partner in crime. You did an outstanding job with all of the graphic design for the print copy of this book; I am incredibly thankful for your collaboration.

Jess, my rockstar of an editor, thank you for your patience and diligence with this project!

Anna, my long-time friend and writing comrade, thank you for also giving this book an overview and assuring me that it did, in fact, make sense.

To my Sisterhood group and the countless friends who cheered me on and told me not to quit; you saved this book on numerous occasions.

Finally, to my father. You have constantly reflected the love of my Heavenly Father to me. Thank you for never giving up on me; I hope I did you proud.

Photography by Aurora Grace

ABOUT THE AUTHOR

Annis Would is the nom de plume of Annis Nelson. After the common response to her adventure stories became "Yes, well, Annis *would*,"her friends gave her a hashtag which is now a rather fitting penname.

An adventurer, hobbyist chef and long-time writer, she is feeling a considerable amount of emotions at having completed her first book—almost as many as she has about writing about herself in the third person. When she isn't traveling or writing, she can often be found in a kitchen preparing to feed friends and family.

The author can be found on Instagram, Twitter and Facebook @anniswould. As of publication, she posts a Facebook Live video every Monday, Wednesday and Friday. Her website is anniswould.com.